NEVER SELL YOUR FIRST HOME

Never Sell Your First Home

A Guide for Turning Your Current Home into Your Next, Best Investment

Brendan C. Donelson

Table of Contents

WHY THIS BOOK NOW?

The title of this book hurts a little every time I say it. That's because I learned the truth of it the hard way—after I had sold my first home. If I still owned that house today, I'd be roughly a half-million dollars richer than I am . . . or maybe more.

If that sounds like a wake-up call to you, read on. I hope to spare you the same cringe-worthy results, and if you're already past the point of no return (your first house is long gone), don't despair. I have some good news and great suggestions for you, too.

Planning for a (Bright!) Future

This book is born of necessity. It's not a byproduct of simply wanting to be an author or to position myself as an authority. I'm writing this book because too many people need help, and I don't have time to meet with everyone. But I truly wish I could.

I feel an urgency about writing because I know that if the ideas in this book had been published sooner, it could have improved someone's net worth significantly or maybe even changed the course of his or her life. If I had written this five or ten years ago and caused someone to keep their first home, that person's financial well-being would have been far, far better than it is now! No matter who they are, regardless of where they live, and whatever of the size of their first home, they would be better off if they had not sold it! And knowing this makes me nauseous. No one should have to lose that way in real estate.

I want you to be someone whose financial well-being multiplies greatly because this is in your hands. To that end, I'm willing to share every strategy and method I've learned in more than two decades of financing real estate transactions.

Since 1995, I've been gathering data and learning from clients whom I've helped with their mortgages. The market gyrations during that time have given me a breadth of experience I would never have imagined when I first started my career. But as a result, I've learned approaches that apply in just about every type of housing market there is. In this book, I share what I've learned from hundreds of client engagements so you can educate yourself about how you can— and why you should!—own income-producing investment property.

You may know that real estate investing has the potential to provide a lifestyle most people only dream of. Countless "how to" books, TV shows, podcasts, and webinars belch strategies and systems "guaranteed" to make you a fortune.

But you also may suspect that it's not quite as easy as they make it look.

And that's where I can really help. You see, I'm a realist. I know what works, and even better, I know what can work for you. At the risk of sounding boastful (okay . . . I actually am being boastful here), I have yet to meet or encounter a client who has shown me any better ways to own income-producing real estate than what I will share with you.

Writing in Quiet

As I write this, I'm sitting in the dining room of a vacation rental property I own on Monument Avenue in Charlestown, Massachusetts, a charming community near downtown Boston. My youngest son is decked out in a new Celtics jersey and watching the Simpsons in the next room. My two older boys are still asleep, and my wife is drinking coffee, catching up with work on her phone, and sorting through inquiries on properties we own and manage as short-term rentals back in Nashville. I just returned from a stroll to a neighborhood bakery to grab croissants, some sparkling water, and a cigar. (I haven't smoked one in years, but I feel like celebrating life right now!)

My idyllic quiet time has prodded me towards (at long last) writing this book. I've had enough of keeping this information to myself and being able to share it with only those clients who actually visit my office. From the folks I've served through the years, I've heard echoes of *Never Sell Your First Home* a thousand times. I've outlined hundreds of solutions for clients who ask about keeping their homes or when they lament having sold one or more of their previous homes.

Over the past decade, I've held countless meetings—often lasting a couple of hours or more—just to get every detail itemized. I have two dry-erase boards that have served as my canvas to map out client situations. Circles, arrows, and squiggly lines connect the dots for the people I work with, and the meetings typically end with a client saying, "Do you mind if I take a picture of this so I can study it." The drawings become their own, personal map toward building wealth (getting richer!) through owning a portfolio of real estate.

I've had many "I'm going write it one day soon" moments, so why exactly now? I can tell you precisely.

It's because of my college roommate and dear friend who, with his wife, bought their first home at 29 Harvard Street, here in Charlestown, Massachusetts—exactly three blocks away! On my walk to get croissants and the cigar, I remembered their situation.

My friends went through some incredible twists and turns, probably should have kept their property forever, but like me, got confused by all they were facing, and ended up selling their first home. You see, perhaps if I had written this sooner, I could have helped them, too. (Audible sigh.) So, hopefully, by the time you're finished reading *Never Sell Your First Home*, you'll be completely prepared to . . .

Do What I Didn't

Okay. Let me back off my premise—but just a little bit.

If you're feeling dejected because you've already sold your first home, the news may not be all bad. In some (rare) cases, selling your first home can actually be the right thing to do. The "never" on the cover of this book doesn't apply to everybody all the time. But on this point, I won't waver: It absolutely does apply to most people, most of the time, and I'd like to show how you almost certainly are one of them.

While there can be good reasons to sell the home you live in, that wasn't the case for me. In fact, the 20/20 hindsight is so clear that it makes a great—if a bit painful—story. It's the bottom line that hurts so much. As I said, if I hadn't sold my first home, I would be a half-million dollars richer right now than I am. That's $500,000 wealthier than I am if I still owned that house! Not only that, I would also be cash-flowing $30,000 a year! Yowch! I don't even like to think about what I might do if I had an extra $30,000 every year!

Part of the problem I faced was that, when the decision to move surfaced for me, there were no resources like this to help with the questions I had. Most real estate advice at the time was about flipping houses or acquiring foreclosures and tax-sale properties. The pages ahead are aimed to fill the void. My simple mission is that no one, when deciding to sell or keep their current home, makes an uninformed decision or a decision based on fear of the unknown.

Deals, Deals and More Deals

Every week, my work teaches me new things about acquiring property—whether a primary home, a second home, or investment properties. I've also learned a lot through my personal real estate deals. At this point, I own the house I live in, 15 rental properties, and have construction underway on an 8-unit mixed commercial/residential use building. I've also been part of 14 other-home acquisitions and subsequent sales just for myself. So, all together, that's 40 personal real estate deals.

Acquiring and retaining these properties has afforded me firsthand aches and pains, so I hope you'll learn from my experience instead of enduring all the problems yourself. While this experience doesn't make me the world's leading expert, it's enough to know strategies that work and others that don't. The blend of hands-on experience, client interaction, and personal transactions that I bring to the table is the right combination to provide some high-potency learning for you.

My client stories provide unbiased and unfiltered data. Through them, I simply show examples of what did—or could likely—happen in real-life situations. They'll really expand your understanding, so I encourage you to read them. Even if you're not a "numbers guy" or "gal," the situations are extremely valuable to review and possibly use to help you make a decision on your next real estate opportunity.

As we get started, I congratulate you for taking the time to invest in yourself. I've found that investing in myself first always makes my other investments pay off better. While many books about real estate offer great tips to help you on your journey to success, I've found some gems about how to do real estate that other folks overlook. I'll cover the fundamentals you need, no matter what your long-term strategies may be, and then I'll guide you through how to make one of the easiest-to-implement but seldom done investments pay off big for you. Whether you're a first-time homeowner or way down the homeowner path, I hope you'll enjoy all the angles and scenarios I've got for you. So, let's go make your future bright!

A Note on How to Use This Book

I've created space in the book to write things down. That's because books that have had the most impact on me are the ones in which I took lots of notes and jotted down thoughts the author inspired.

Dan Kennedy wrote *No B.S. Time Management for Entrepreneurs: The Ultimate No Holds Barred Kick Butt Take No Prisoners Guide to Time Productivity and Sanity* in which he shared a blank form that the reader could complete to help understand what his or her time is worth. When I read Dan's book, I wrote down what my hourly time was worth based on my income goal for that year. And that number is still a critical reminder and planning tool for me today, 15 years later.

So, please have a pen ready to write your thoughts and answer the questions I pose.

Written memory is a powerful thing.

Chapter 1

How Can This Book Help You?

Although you've probably never thought about it exactly this way, you're in one of four different real estate circumstances that each requires a specific approach to make the most of your opportunities. Your first step is to identify which situation you are in. Then you can create the optimal strategy for yourself. So, read through the four options below and decide which sounds the most like you.

a.bacall

"Welcome to Shouda, Wouda, Couda, the investment hindsight show."

"The Rookie"

You've owned your first home for a while and aren't sure what to do right now.

You own your first home and possibly want to move and are considering keeping your first as a rental. You're on the fence, and may be a little scared, so selling it, taking the equity, and putting it into another property sounds easy. This also seems to make sense because you want lower payments on your next home or maybe want to use some of the money from the sale to pay off other debts or buy new furniture for the next house. The equity in your current place might be an opportunity to simplify your life as well. The idea of having a bigger pile of money in the bank sounds nice. Other "fear factors" may also be in play. For instance, you're afraid of the risks of keeping the house because your home may have maintenance issues, or perhaps being a landlord just sounds hard.

But you also recognize the potential flip side: Keeping it!

The idea of keeping your place is appealing in the long-term, and your gut is somehow telling you that it might make really good financial sense. You've heard about owning rental properties and know that investing in real estate versus putting money into the stock market is a good idea. And: The idea of having someone else pay down your mortgage while you live somewhere else sounds pretty cool! Not only that, having the home increase in value at the same time sounds even better! And you are fairly confident that the neighborhood and area is on the up and up.

If this resonates with you and you've hoped for a resource to educate yourself and possibly build a case for keeping your home as a rental, property, I've got some really good news for you. I call them Pro Tips.

 Here are my Pro Tips and immediate action steps for you:

Read all the chapters with funny sounding stories! See which one of them best matches your current situation.

Read the detailed steps on turning your home into a rental property (Chapter 4) and fill in the worksheets to help you evaluate whether or not to keep the house.

Post your question on the NSYFH Facebook page or website NeverSellYourFirstHome. com in the Comments section. You can contact us about your specific situation, and we may be able to provide additional insight or resources to help you make a sound decision moving forward, because we know: There are a lot of variables to consider!

"The Regrettor"

You owned your first home and sold it! You regret that decision and don't want it to happen again. You might own again and are preparing for a future move.

Like me, the title of this book probably strikes a nerve for you! You often remind yourself just how much more that first house of yours is worth today. You knew, deep down, you should probably have kept your house, but no one was encouraging you to do that, so you went against your instincts and sold it. Your situation might have ended up differently if even just one person had encouraged you. Or if there had only been a book "lighthouse" to shine the way on your voyage. A book like this could have shown you just how uncomplicated being a landlord can be. A few tips, case studies, planning worksheets, or sample leases would have helped you with your decision to keep that property. And who knows? That home may almost have been paid off by now, and with solid cash flow you, would have been earning another $20,000 year while sitting on your couch.

But it didn't happen that way!

That was then; this is now. No need to beat yourself up anymore at this point! Because . . . if you own now, you can turn this house into a rental property and go find yourself a new place to live!

 Here are my Pro Tips and immediate action steps for you:

Use this book as a guide to never sell your current home or the next home you buy.

Identify the stories that relate to your situation.

Tell us why you sold your first home, so we can help you think through your situation this time around. What was your critical moment when you turned left instead of right?

Or simply reach out to us with a question you have about your situation now.

To help others: Recommend this book to a friend or loved one or keep a copy so your children can read it when they buy their first home.

"The Dreamer"

You don't own yet but are thinking about buying someday. In fact, owning multiple properties appeals to you, and turning your first home into an investment property at some point sounds smart.

You're thinking about all the possible ways to become wealthy when you get older. The idea of having your own Monopoly ™ board filled with real estate is exciting. You'd like to be a little more educated on the entire real estate game, and this book can fit on your tool belt.

For a great start, read the details in Chapter 3

on acquiring your first home as an "Owner Occupied" property. Browse our website (NeverSellyourFirstHome.com), and ask yourself questions as hypothetical scenarios come to mind. Educating yourself now about real estate will pay off later. Taking action once you have the knowledge is exciting, satisfying, and profitable!

 Here are my Pro Tips and immediate action steps for you:

As you read this book and peruse our website, take notes on questions you have.

Go ahead and reach out to a professional. At NSYFH, we're here to answer questions to the best of our ability in 24 hours.

Pay special attention to the stories and read the owner's suggestions.

Don't sell my first home ☐

"The Researcher"

Maybe you're a financial planner or a consultant and have clients who are investors. That means you need to know how to talk the talk or provide valuable advice or direction about real estate and mortgages.

Besides being helpful for you personally, this book can sharpen your saw in areas where you might not spend much time or have working knowledge. Eventually, almost everyone invests in real estate, and meanwhile, many people dream about owning real estate. And when clients come to you with their next "crazy" real estate idea, you'd like to be in control of your thoughts and have as much knowledge and advice so as to offer them a solution.

Look no further!

You like researching things as a way to be a valuable and trusted advisor whenever called upon, and this book is likely the tool you need. Read it through and familiarize yourself with the stories. Look at the pictures and worksheets. You'll glean some usable ideas and learn the lingo about real estate and mortgages. You may even see connections between the case studies and create your own scenarios to share! For sure, the book can be a reference for you as situations come to your attention, and, at times, you may want to give it to clients or others in your inner circle of experts.

 Here are my Pro Tips and immediate action steps for you:

Contact us whenever you have a question regarding any of the material we've provided.

Purchase this book for your clients or send them selections from it. I believe you'll be able to provide superior financial planning with this as a tool in your belt.

Client: _____

Friend: _____

Review the case studies in the book and on our website for a refresher when a client calls you for advice. And when a specific question arises from someone you're working with, let us know what's up. We're glad to help by reviewing specific case studies or to offer advice for your particular situation.

You know who you are!

☐ **The Rookie**   ☐ **The Regrettor**

☐ **The Dreamer**   ☐ **The Researcher**

Now that you've identified who you are, this guide applies to your specific real estate situation. Lastly, here are a few quick suggestions that apply to everyone.

1. Write notes in the book! And answer the questions!

Did you answer the question above about who you are?

2. Ask friends who sold their first home

about their situations. Your friends may have sold their first home and could provide first-hand knowledge about their decision.

3. Ask us a question any time. Our website is the easiest way to ask a question, or you can reach us through Facebook at the *Never Sell Your First Home* fan page.

Chapter 2

WHOA! I Sold My First Home!

It might cross your mind to wonder why you should read a book from someone who made the very mistake he's now advising you not to make. Why should I be the one to offer advice?

Honestly, I wondered the same thing for a few years, but I got over it. ☺ For one thing, I learned a lot from my failure! But I was also pre-disposed to eventually "do the right thing," even if it took a while.

"Study Henderson's career closely. He's made all the mistakes so you don't have to."

Getting from There to Here

Growing up, I was excited to have any kind of paying job and always felt an entrepreneurial spirit inside. In the fourth grade, I started mowing lawns with my neighbor, Neil. We pushed our mowers around the cul-de-sac, knocking on doors and asking to mow the neighbors' yards.

On our way to success, we had six or seven yards we mowed regularly. Then we branched out by riding our bikes to clients in neighborhoods further away. We created a promotional flyer for B&N Lawn Care and eventually were servicing a whopping 15 or 20 yards.

Typically, we got paid in cash, my half of which I would crumple into my pockets. Riding the bike, with one hand on the handlebar and the other hauling the lawn mower backwards along the road, I would peddle home. Once there, I took the scrambled bills, sprayed fabric starch on them, and ironed them flat on my Mom's ironing board. The clean, crispy money smelled wonderful as I placed them reverently into a little red metal box—my "CASHBOX." I still remember how happy that fabric-starch, fresh smell made me!

In ninth grade, I went to work for Vienna Seafood, my brother's best friend's seafood company. A small retail shop, Vienna featured a live lobster tank, truly fresh fish and shrimp, and live Maryland crabs. The loader and unloader of fish, crustaceans, and store supplies, I also helped set up the shop and arrange fish in storage cases. In the process, I learned to fillet fish, handle lobsters and crabs without getting pincered, work the cash register, and help clients decide which fish or seafood they wanted for dinner.

Working in a highly personal, family-owned business meant a lot to me. The owners cared about details. They made New England clam chowder from scratch, their own cocktail sauce and crab cakes, and had a library of unique recipes on how to cook fish.

One of the perks of my job was taking home fish the owners gave me. I tried all sorts of ways to grill or cook tuna, flounder, salmon, shark, sole, and more.

At the store, Christmastime and the Fourth of July were the busiest times of the year. Lines would form outside the store, stressing us out for hours on end, trying to keep up. Some days didn't wrap up until 10:00 or 11:00 PM, and I would get home stinking like a fish and worn out from standing for ten hours. But the worst part of the job was having to wear wet gloves that let water soak through to my skin. It made my hands break out and look like I had leprosy. ☺ Still, that job taught me a lot. I worked there all through high school and up to my freshman year in college.

As if the fishy job weren't enough, I also

started painting houses for a company called College Pro Painters (even though I was in high school at the time). It was a loosely run franchise that trained workers to bid and paint jobs on residential houses.

Once I learned bidding, I knew I could start my own painting company and get clients through word of mouth or door knocking. So, I branched out and realized that running my own painting service was more fun because I could be my own boss and manage my schedule the way I wanted. My experience knocking on doors for the mowing business served me well since the same tactic worked for building a painting business, too.

Nostalgia Time:

What was one of your early jobs, and what did it teach you?

I ended up with so much work that I hired some buddies to help me. The business paid well, but painting houses outside in the hot, muggy summer stinks almost as bad as fish! And there were mountains of details to keep track of—setting up, prepping the areas to paint, cleaning up every day at the end. Painting houses also teaches you other fun things like how to avoid bees on ladders, wasp nests under the eaves, how to place ladders safely on sloped areas around the house, and what to do with spots where you risk life and limb to reach with your roller or paintbrush.

One part I especially enjoyed, though, was the satisfaction of seeing what a house looked like before and after I was done. It was way gratifying to make clients happy with my work. Some even wanted to pay me extra "tips" because they so appreciated what I had done.

My junior summer in college, I continued to paint houses during the day and began waiting tables at night at a fine DC-area restaurant called L'Auberge Chez Francois. (At my interview, it helped that I could speak a little French.)

For my first week, I trained under the head waiter, James, who managed a total wait staff of 20 people. After that, serving clients in a famous, high-end restaurant taught me the extremely useful skill of reading body language.

One of the first tables I served was for a famous politician and government official. Af-

ter getting over the jitters, I realized the folks were just there to eat, and I simply needed to do what James had trained me to do. Even though I only worked at L'Auberge Chez Francois for 12 weeks, the discipline of keeping things clean, serving people promptly and politely, "reading between the lines" of what clients want, and managing a wild assortment of details are lessons I still value.

I graduated college with a degree in history but wanted to do something with numbers. Go figure! In fact, the idea of working on Wall Street sounded awesome to me. Since a bunch of my friends were taking jobs in New York, I trekked up to The Big Apple, and managed to land a job at NYMEX, the New York Mercantile Exchange, as a clerk for an options trading firm.

To get the job, I went through a seriously unconventional interview in which they asked me about all sorts of random calculations and how I would solve them. Fortunately, in spite of my history degree, being good in math came naturally to me. My father had been an undergraduate math major at Yale and went on to get two PhD's—one in math from Stanford, the other in physics from Johns Hopkins. I must have absorbed knowledge by some sort of osmosis from the large books on the dinner table about quantum mechanics. (The symbols inside looked like a foreign language.) Add to that my mother's art business of doing house portraits and writing motivational books, and I guess I was primed for being a numbers-oriented, creative, entrepreneurial, book-writing, real estate rogue. Whew!

For the trading firm, I worked in the World Trade Center, Tower 1 (yes, really). We started every day at 6:00 AM and jammed straight through until 6:00 PM. I learned options trading, the significance of volatility, and how to hedge trades by buying or selling futures.

 Although the job was exciting at first, I realized quickly that it was not for me in the long run. The culture was way too cutthroat for my taste. Everyone seemed out for themselves and ready to turn you in if you didn't follow orders. I lasted four months, three weeks, and two days (but who's counting?) before I walked away.

Even though NYMEX wasn't the right fit for me, I knew I wanted to be out in the world, meeting people and selling something. I just didn't know what.

So, I did what any unemployed, 20-something would do—moved back to Virginia and to my old bedroom at my parent's house, right? Ha! Can you say, "Bad move"? Within a week, I was beyond stir crazy!

But then something special began to take shape. One of my sister's friends was a mortgage broker at his own company, and at the same time, my first cousin was a mortgage banker at a bank. Intrigued, I started shadowing my sister's friend at his office, but it was chaos. Based on the number of angry calls I had to answer from his clients, I learned that this guy could not be trusted. People constantly called the office looking for him, and my job was to intercept them and try to make sense of why they were so angry. It turns out my sister's friend was very bad at telling the truth,

and time and time again, he seriously overprom-
ised people—and underdelivered!

After just a few weeks, I left him and began
working alongside my cousin at the established
mortgage bank where the environment could
hardly have been more different. We wore suits
and ties every day, and I received two solid weeks
of formal training. My job focused on meeting
with real estate agents, builders, bank clients, and
anyone else who could possibly need our services.
(Do you see a theme developing here?)

We had many ways to find clients, and to me,
this was the best part of the business. Some tech-
niques were really creative. For instance, I have
fond memories teaching homebuyer seminars
in the basement of the Pentagon with a retired,
former-military realtor. We helped enlisted men
learn the ins-and-outs of buying a house.

*What were you doing when you
started to see the pieces of your
career come together?*

The business was a great fit for me. I learned
something new every day as my cousin and I dis-
cussed each other's game plans. After six months,
I began getting consistent referrals from real estate agents, financial planners, builders, and past
clients who had enjoyed working with me. (They
liked me! Cool!)

Since I was making a little more money than before, I moved in with a friend who was a financial advisor in Washington, DC. Although our "home" was a rundown house on N Street in Georgetown, my rent was only $400 per month—a just-right, super-cheap rate for two young professionals trying to figure out their careers.

Every day brought welcome challenges—reviewing credit reports, analyzing income tax returns, evaluating net worth statements, divorce decrees, bankruptcy documents, and bank and asset statements of all types. Understanding these fundamentals became the backdrop for what I know about finance, budgeting, saving money, investing in real estate, and the building blocks for financial success.

In the mortgage business, I become intimately acquainted with the realities of personal finance. I got the "inside story," like the fact that people who live in big houses often have big loans against those houses. Before that, I had thought only rich people lived in large houses and that if someone was driving a super nice car, he or she must be rich, too! Can you say, "Not true"?

As my mortgage business grew, I reviewed the financial circumstances of more and more people and saw a lot of crazy patterns. Most people were living (way) beyond their means and had almost no cash available. It was not fun to be the one to tell clients how bad off their finances were. At other times, it was refreshing to see how resourceful people could be and how willing to save money. Every situation was unique, and that kept my job enjoyable.

Through on-the-job "training" by clients, I learned what to do and what not to do. I saw different levels of success—and different levels of failure. Meeting clients with a variety of income sources (salary, commission, self-employed, trust-fund babies, even some unemployed) gave me immense perspective on my own situation.

There are very few jobs that allow you to go from zero knowledge about a person's finances to knowing everything about them within an hour or two, but my job was one of them. Credit reports, bank statements, tax returns, pay stubs, divorce decrees, alimony agreements, asset statements, 401k and IRA accounts, bankruptcy documents, disability awards letters, gift documents from family members, trust agreements, VA benefits, corporate tax returns, and rental property leases are incredibly revealing!

No one in any other professional finance field (financial consultants, CPA's, or attorneys) is required to look at as much personal information about a client as we do in mortgage lending. At some point in a client relationship, others might get to our level of detail, but in our profession, it's required from the start, and it has to be reviewed in a compressed period of time. That's one of the greatest hidden benefits of being a mortgage lender! Acquiring this knowledge allowed me to make some amazingly good financial decisions for myself.

In 1997, for instance, a fascinating client of mine named Mr. Cook showed me the world of owning rental property. A successful attorney who owned his principal residence in Langley, Virginia, he also owned rental properties around the US—one in Jackson, Wyoming, and another in San Francisco, California. In rearranging his debt to improve his cash flow, I ended up helping him refinance all three properties.

When was the first time someone piqued your interest in owning investment property?

Mr. Cook was mine.

While working on Mr. Cook's deals, he educated me about fundamentals of property location and time value. I still remember something specific he told me about the property he owned in the Knob Hill District of San Francisco: "Brendan, they're never going to create more land in San Francisco! My wife would love for me to sell this property and pocket the cash or pay off our current home mortgage here in Virginia, but I'm never selling it. I get $3,000 per month rent [even though it was under rent control in the city], but it's the location that will always be valuable!" Nearly 20 years after telling me this, he eventually did sell the property, and at that point, his gains became a great part of his retirement strategy.

Mr. Cook's never-create-more-land concept made sense to me. He also told me the price he paid for his various properties and where each city's real estate market had been. The markets had been somewhat of a roller coaster, but he explained the value of time, coupled with location and scarcity of land. Overall, he more than quadrupled his equity in the properties, all while cash-flowing positively. He was both making an income and increasing his net worth at the same time, seemingly without much effort.

Wow, did this really make sense to me! I felt like Luke Skywalker getting trained in the swamp by Yoda.

The Gem That Was Sold

In May 1998, shortly after working with Yoda—I mean, Mr. Cook—I wrote an offer to buy my first home. The address was 1304 Roundhouse Lane, Apt. 304, in Alexandria, Virginia. The building looked like a college dorm but my girlfriend Christina (now my wife) and I toured the model home and thought it was beautiful. After sitting down with the onsite agent and choosing our upgrades, we ended up with a contract on the condo for $209,000.

To do the deal, we had to put five percent down. At the time, 30-year, fixed rates were around 8.5 percent. Being in the industry, I looked at all sorts of products and decided to roll the dice and chose a one-year adjustable-rate loan with a starting rate of 7.25 percent, and it worked well for us. The new mortgage was $1,650 for principal, interest, taxes, and PMI (private mortgage insurance), plus a condo fee of $300 a month. In all, the payment was $1,950 and change. Although it seemed like a lot to me at the time, Christina's previous rent was $900 and mine was $500. Since we were both working, it wasn't crazy to have a new total payment of $1,950 versus our previous combined total of $1,400 in rent.

During the four or five months it took to finish the building, we often drove by to check on progress and began meeting people who lived nearby. There were some interesting folks in the neighborhood—a morning radio DJ, his wife, and their bulldog, also a few salespeople from the subdivision.

We closed on the home in September 1998, as soon as the construction was complete. Then, a problem developed. We began to feel that life in DC was a rat race, and we wanted to leave.

The previous year, we had attended two family weddings—one in Nashville for my cousin and the other in Ft. Worth for my wife's cousin—and when we came back to DC after visiting a smaller city like Nashville, we felt empty. In fact, we were downright depressed. Not a great feeling when you've just bought your first house.

We both wanted to start over somewhere new, but we had just closed on the condo six months before! After thinking through our options, we picked Nashville as the place we wanted to live. Since we owned a house in Virginia, though, we had to figure out what to do if we were to move to Tennessee.

Have you ever wanted "a fresh start" but didn't know how to make it happen?

Our new-home community was run by an HOA (homeowners association), and at the time, the original contractor had two more buildings to put up. That meant, if we were going to sell, the builder immediately became our competition. Knowing this, my initial gut reaction was to meet with the onsite agent who had sold us our home and see what he thought we could sell our home for. To my surprise, the agent said our property would be easy to sell because the inventory of new buildings wouldn't be complete for another four or five months. People regularly toured the model unit who wanted a place in less time than that, and he was constantly turning them away. Most didn't come back because they needed to move sooner. So, he told me he would send me anyone who came in. It sounded promising, to say the least!

After meeting with him, I strolled back to our condo, though, thinking about the rental rates for our property if we couldn't sell it. We had secured a 2-bedroom rental in Nashville for $1200 per month, and the idea of having two obligations (my current mortgage and the new rent) made me nervous. I knew nothing about owning a rental property, but after a little research, I discovered that people would likely rent our property for somewhere around $2,000 per month—barely enough to cover our mortgage payment plus condo fee. The good news was that our mortgage payment included principal reduction of about $250 per month, but we would not be cash flow positive if we were to pay a property manager.

> That was the moment I stopped thinking about keeping our property.

I had no resources to explain the potential benefits. There was no such thing as a Google search button where I could type "converting my current home into a rental property" or "becoming a landlord" or "rental property 101" or "how to be a landlord from out of state." Also, I didn't grasp the basic concepts of rental contracts, how to collect rent, what to do if something breaks, and so on. Even though the property was practically brand new and had a condominium association managing the exterior and grounds, becoming a property manager and landlord was something I didn't think I was qualified to do. In my mind, the risks far outweighed the rewards.

So . . . I decided to sell our house and pocket the (immediate) money. It was the "standard conclusion" for folks in our situation: *The equity in our home would become the down payment when I was ready to buy our next house, in Nashville.*

Although I thought the choice made sense given our pressure-filled and nerve-wracking situation, my decision started haunting me about three or four years later. Flash forward to now (see the summary below) and my annual rental income after maintenance and expenses would have easily been $12,000 per year minimum.

Roundhouse Knockout

The Facts

Address:
Roundhouse Lane,
Alexandria, VA

Property Type:
Condominium

Monthly Mortgage Payment:
$1,950 (including a montly
condo fee)

The Situation

I thought I needed the money
I had in the home for savings,
and eventually a new home
down payment. I was nervous
about leaving money in a real
estate investment and moving
600 miles away.

The Details

Today's Value: $725,000

Current Rent in Its Market: $3,100

Mortgage Balance:

1998
Value: $209,500
Mortgage: $193,000

1999
Value: $240,000
Mortgage: $191,000

2021
Value: $725,000
Mortgage would have
been: $78,000

 ## The Bottom Line

Selling this property was a mistake.

Approximate net worth impact: -$500,000

Chapter 3

Your First Home Purchase and What Makes It so Important

And the 197 Details ☺ that Go into It

Before understanding how to turn your first—or next—home into a thriving rental property, it's vital to set the stage for why it might be a good idea. There's no better way to do that than by evaluating what went into buying your first home. Understanding the reasons for making that decision if you don't currently own or understanding all the reasons and processes that went into that decision if you do own, will give you a solid foundation for moving forward.

"We're looking for a traditional suburban neighborhood with all the urban amenitites."

It Only Happens Once

For most people, their first home purchase is a memorable experience and had been on their bucket list in their twenties or thirties. Typically, it feels like an enormous undertaking and monumental decision.

In meetings or on the phone, I've explained to thousands of first-time buyers the basics of home ownership. I've taught more than 100 homebuyer classes and developed printed materials outlining the details of who does what during the process. I've created a 52-page slide presentation called Homebuyer 101, and I've counseled thousands who were moving a second or third time. With others in my company, I've taught investment property seminars and consulted with loan officers around the country who have assisted tens of thousands of clients, collectively. After all of this, I've noticed that people who purchase their first home generally do so for one of the five reasons outlined below.

The Five Reasons You Buy Your First Home

1. The RENT vs. OWN A-Ha moment!

They run the numbers on renting versus owning and see that it's clearly more advantageous to own. They're also tired of doing their taxes every year and not having any significant deductions, they have enough money for a down payment, and they feel ready to take on the responsibility. Their money has been going down the rent drain for too long. An economic analysis says it's time to buy.

2. Sick and tired!

They got sick and tired of their current renting situation because they were constantly moving or confronting oversized, uncaring management companies. Worse, they might have had a bad experience with a neighbor in the building where they rented or unpleasant encounters with their landlord. They weren't sure they were ready to own, but circumstances pushed in that direction and suddenly, the idea of buying their first home gave them a sense of pride, independence, or belonging someplace. They wanted the security of not having to move again; they wanted a place to call home.

3. Born to own

These are planners or analyzers and for them, owning a home has, for a long time, been a foregone conclusion. They've created a savings plan for the down payment and established an affordable range in which to buy. For them, the process usually took between 6 and 18 months to execute from the day they started. They followed a well-defined process and timeline, similar to the one I outline later in this chapter.

4. I love my neighborhood

They love a specific area of town and want to live there. They might have friends or family who live in that neighborhood. The schools are a perfect fit for their children. They like the nearby restaurants or other amenities, and they had decided that when the opportunity came up to buy in that particular area, they would jump on it!

5. Epiphany or random genius

They inadvertently came to the decision to buy a home. Attending a friend's house-warming party might have been a trigger. Or they stopped at an open house because they saw a sign in the neighborhood one weekend. Or for some, there's no identifiable catalyst. They just "arrived" at wanting to own through conversations or on an impulse. I often liken these people to the ones who go out for a cup of coffee and come home with a new dog!

Which reason caused you to buy your first home?

Regardless of how and why you decided to buy your first home, once the decision is reached, most buyers then hone their house "wish list" and have specific answers for the standard realtor questions.

I/we decided to buy our first home because of reason # _____

_____

_____

Tell your story to yourself here: _____

_____

_____

_____

_____

_____

_____

_____

_____

_____

_____

_____

Your Why's: A Self-Evaluation Checklist

Here are some of the typical questions you ask yourself when shopping for a house:

- What type of home do I want? (townhouse, single family, condo, farm, or other)

- What architectural style do I like? (Tudor, ranch, bungalow, modern, cottage, loft)

- Where do I want to live? (the city, suburbs, a planned neighborhood, a rural property)

- What layout do I like? (open floor plan, split level, loft style, two story, basement)

- What kind of storage do I need? (number of closets, shelving, attic space)

- What number and size of bedrooms do I need?

- What number of bathrooms do I need? (size of bathrooms, master bath qualities, and other baths/showers/toilets)

- What kitchen layout and design do I like? (quality of appliances, countertops, storage)

- What's the condition of property? (when it was built, condition of interior, exterior, updates)

- What maintenance is required for: windows, doors, HVAC system, roof?

- Is there a basement? Is it finished?

- Is there a garage? (one-car, two-car, storage)

- What is the yard and landscaping like? (how much to take care of, fences, how big is the yard)

- Are there outdoor spaces? (patios and screened-in porches)

- What are the surrounding homes and properties like? Is this area getting better, or is it in decline?

- What are the safety issues? Is there crime in the area? Does the property have an alarm system?

- What amenities does the area offer? Where can I eat? Shop? Ride my bike? Take walks?

- What's the school system like? Ratings and any special programs offered?

- How far is it from work? How long will my commute be from there? What is the traffic like?

- What happens when family visits? (handicap accessibility, guest beds/baths)

- Are there any additional costs/amenities? Is the property located in an HOA or condo that could have a pool, common area or other type of communal space? If so, are there homeowner fees associated with the property?

BD OBSERVATION

Whether or not you're conscious of these questions or notice these things, your subconscious is evaluating all the details. Because you want to live in the home, instinctively your mind processes these things, and that results in a "feeling" about the place. Becoming conscious of these details, though, is important and the information critical to use later when making your decision to sell or to keep the property and rent it out. If you've never owned a home, these details are essential when you begin your search. If you do own, this list is a good reminder of all the trial and error and work that went into making your decision to buy in the first place.

What made you buy your first home?
(list 5 things)

1. _____

2. _____

3. _____

4. _____

5. _____

A wise man once told me that every homebuyer has three basic needs:

1. To see houses
2. To understand the process
3. To get their money right (understand their mortgage)

Particularly if you are a Rookie or Dreamer, this is great to know. If you are a Regrettor or Researcher, this will be an excellent refresher of the process you went through.

Once you have the general process in mind, it's important to know how each step plays out. To help you with that, I've detailed below a list of items that play into a typical process for buying a home.

The 10 Steps for Successfully Buying Your First Home

1. Decide you want to be a homeowner.

• Evaluate which of the five typical reasons stated above apply to you. Whichever it is, you're ready to own and want to get started.

2. Assemble your team.

A. Find the best real estate agent for you.

• Pick a realtor you feel comfortable with.

You'll be working with this person for a while, and even though their experience can be helpful, it's important that you don't place too much value on how long they've been in the business. First and foremost, choose someone relatable and real.

- Review Buyer's Agent agreement.
- Complete Buyer Needs list (schools, yard, bedrooms, etc.).
- Assess availability of homes based on what you can afford.

B. Find a lender and study your loan options (you might ask your realtor to refer a lender they trust).

- Pick a bank or mortgage lender you feel comfortable with. Remember that you will also be working with this person for a while. As with a realtor, their experience will help, but, again, you want to choose someone you relate to well.
- Review your credit, income, and assets.
- Complete Rent vs. Own/Move Up Buyer Analysis.
- Uncover what you can afford with Your Mortgage Scale.
- Get formally pre-approved or become a "certified buyer."

3. Start looking.

- Preview neighborhoods, styles, and surrounding amenities.
- Set appointments to see homes that meet your criteria.
- Set up second showings on homes of particular interest to you.

4. Make an offer.

- Have your agent write an official offer.
- Review the real estate sales contract.
- Submit an earnest money deposit.
- Wait for your agent and the seller's agent to negotiate (takes 24 to 48 hours).
- Review your numbers with the lender, prep approval letter, and communicate with your agent on variables.

5. Your offer gets accepted.

- Secure final acceptance of your offer from the seller (if not, return to "Start looking").
- Set a date for home inspection (normally within five days of offer acceptance).
- Lock-in loan terms and sign documents for your mortgage.

- Lender orders appraisal to confirm the value of the home.

6. Renegotiate contract terms, if inspection or appraisal have issues.

- Review home inspection report.
- Negotiate minor repairs to be completed by seller.
- Possible price reduction or seller offers to pay closing costs or terminate contract if major items revealed (earnest money deposit returned).
- For low appraisal, renegotiate or terminate.
- If terminated, return to "Start looking."

7. Final loan underwriting.

- Lenders update income figures, debts, or other pertinent items.
- Provide final proof of funds for down payment and closing costs.
- Review complete appraisal.
- Underwriters request additional documents or clarifications for final approval.

8. Finalize closing details.

- Confirm your closing date with the attorney's office.

- Lender checks for changes in credit, assets, and employment 72 hours prior to closing.

9. Receive closing document (CD) from lender and closing attorney.

- Check all final mortgage terms.
- Ensure accuracy at least three days prior to closing date.

10. Show up on closing day.

- Sign loan paperwork.
- Bring funds for closing either by wiring or a certified check.
- Sign title documents.
- Pick up keys for your new home.
- Move in!

Wow! If it's been a while, you might have forgotten all those steps, and if you've never done it before, they can seem a bit overwhelming. But: You can do it!

This timeline can take as little as 20 days, up to several months, or even a year. For most, it boils down to urgency and desire. Typically, once people have made up their minds, it takes about 60 to 90 days to work through this timeline.

It's about the Money

I'm often amazed at how much my clients forget about what went into purchasing their first home. It's been shown that the stress of buying a first home is equivalent to that created by the unexpected loss of a loved one. My own theory is that people don't remember all that went into buying a home specifically because of the stress! They prefer to forget. And, somehow, they may have managed to skip some of the steps I mentioned, but that's certainly not recommended.

The critical, last key to buying your first home is to understand your mortgage. Most first-time buyers borrow money for the purchase, and because they are going to live in the home, this is called "owner-occupied" purchase financing.

The rules for owner-occupied loans are less strict, and the terms are usually the best available. Why?

The answer is simple. Statistics show that, if someone will be living in the home, they have a greater likelihood of making the payments. The old phrase "if you don't pay, you don't get to stay" comes to mind. In short: Loans on owner-occupied homes default less often. This means that "owner-occupied" mortgage loans have better interest rates than "non-owner-occupied" loans.

Rules for owner-occupied loans can allow for as little as three percent down—which means loans are readily available for higher levels of down payment as well, such as 5 to 20 percent down. In addition, the terms are typically fixed for 15 to 30 years, and standard interest rates for loans like these have been between 3.5 and 5.5 percent over the period 2010 to 2018. One caveat, though: For owner-occupied loans with less than 20 percent down, the borrower is usually required to carry mortgage insurance.

Monthly mortgage insurance premiums are based on the borrower's credit score and overall loan-to-value ratio (a function of the down payment). The good news with mortgage insurance is that it is no longer required when you have paid the mortgage down to 80 percent of the original sales price of the home. So, theoretically, most people who have their mortgage for five to seven years see their mortgage insurance drop from their monthly payment. That means their total monthly payment decreases over time!

Because the focus of this book is about making the decision to turn your home into a rental, I'm not going to thoroughly review the ABC's of obtaining a home loan here. Essentially, the best part about the initial financing of your first home (or next one), is that the terms are the best you can receive. This helps the future performance of your investment property if (when!) you decide to keep the home.

HAILEY'S COMET

A schoolteacher relocating from Colorado to Nashville, Hailey had bought her first home in 2010 in Colorado. Her school had been in the area's best school district and so was her home.

The move put her under pressure, though, because she had made an aggressive offer on a house in Nashville, and the seller accepted it. She didn't want to sell her Colorado home because she felt sure its great location could make it worth double the current value in the next five to ten years. She had researched the market and knew it would be a highly desirable rental option for families who couldn't afford to buy but wanted to be in that school district.

It seemed obvious, though, that she needed down payment money from selling her Colorado home to buy the one in Nashville. After all, she had no other funds available. Not only that, she had a fairly compelling offer from her dad. He said he would give her additional money for a down payment but only if she sold her home in Colorado. His reasoning, she said, was that "he thought it would be difficult for me to manage a rental from 1000 miles away."

But . . . she really wanted to keep the house in Colorado. Everything inside her said it was the best choice in the long run. And, like most people in a similar situation, she just didn't know how to make it work.

To her credit, she didn't give up easily. Here's what she did:

1. She called her realtor in Colorado to make sure the property was not listed for sale.

2. Instead, Hailey asked the agent if she could find a renter and handle property management. The agent said 'yes' and asked for 10 percent of monthly rent as a management fee.

3. Hailey went to her bank in Colorado and applied for a Home Equity Line of Credit (HELOC).

4. In just 12 days, the bank approved her for a $35,000 line. (This gave her down payment money for the Nashville house.)

5. The Colorado realtor found a young family looking to be in that school district. They signed a one-year lease and gave a one-month deposit check upon signing.

6. With her lease in place, and the $35,000 HELOC check, Hailey closed on her home in Nashville, 30 days from the date her offer was accepted.

Five years have transpired since Hailey kept her Colorado home, and it's now valued at $415,000—double what she paid for it in 2010!

Hailey's comet took off!

Hailey's Comet

The Facts

Address:
Shady Aspen Drive,
Colorado Springs, CO

Property Type:
Single Family

Monthly Mortgage Payment:
$1,250 (including a HELOC
payment)

The Situation

Hailey needs to relocate to TN
from CO for a career advance-
ment. She currently owns a
home in CO but also wants to
purchase a home in TN. Question: Without selling the CO
home, can she afford to buy in
TN? How can she do this?

The Details

Today's Value: $415,000

Current Rent in Its Market: $2,400

Mortgage Balance:

2010
Value: $199,000
Mortgage: $193,000

2016
Would have sold for:
$270,000
Mortgage balance in
2016: $170,000

2021
Value: $415,000
Remaining Mortgage:
$175,000 (Including
HELOC funds used
to buy next home)

The Bottom Line

The owner's decision to not sell has increased the net
worth by $145,000 and the annual income after
expenses is $6,000.

Chapter 4
AT THE CROSSROAD
Are You Ready to Be a Rental Property Owner/Investor?

When Luke Skywalker left his companions and took R2D2 to the weird planet where Yoda lived, he had to make a decision. Yoda told him, "There's no try, only do."

When you begin the analysis for becoming an investor, everything is new. Much of what you encounter may even be contrary to the way you've always thought. So, this chapter will require a different level of thinking and decision-making that you probably are not used to. Why? Because making the decision to keep your property and become a landlord is counter to

our culture. Percentagewise, very few people own rental property (five to ten percent of Americans).

Typically, when we are "done" with our first home, most of us liquidate it and move on to the next one. By doing so, we're simply following what our families and most friends do. For the next few minutes, though, I encourage you to fight through any urge to skip this information and the questions I'll raise for you. Working through this requires your absolute focus because of the level of detail and monetary calculations required. But if you truly want to discover the best scenario for your financial future, these details matter. Some elements matter more than others, but do your best to work through all of these questions! The answers are critical to your decision!

Thinking It Through

 These are 5 essential elements of your keep-or-not-keep decision:

1. Identify the key reasons you would keep your current home as a rental property.

2. Understand the concept of leveraging equity.

3. Examine how to come up with the down payment for your next home.

4. Determine how to qualify for financing.

5. Decide what you want to move into and the next detailed steps.

To start, look at your current home objectively. Answer the eight questions below.

1. In Chapter 2 you listed out why you bought the home. What would be the top three reasons you want to keep it?

    1. _____

    2. _____

    3. _____

2. What do you owe on your home (mortgage balances)?

_____

_____

3. What would your home sell for today?

_____

4. What do you think this home will be worth in five years? Conservatively, why? (Gut answer; don't over analyze!)

_____

_____

5. Use this formula to determine the current equity in your home:

House Value:_____

X 0.92 (formula assumes 6% agent fees, 1% closing cost, 1% repairs prior to final sale)

Proceeds from sale: _____

LESS:

CurrentMortgages:_____

Net Money To You: _____

6. Now, let's break down your current monthly payment (you can find these numbers on the mortgage statement from your lender.)

Principal: _____

Interest: _____

Taxes: _____

Insurance: _____

HOA Fees: _____

7. How much could you rent your current home for? (Again, don't over analyze; gut answer.)

_____

8. And let's look at your future equity. What will your equity be in five years?

FIRST

Current Mortgage Balance: _____

LESS: Additional Principal Payments:

_____

(Multiply your current monthly principal X 64.5 to account for compound interest and insert the result here.)

Future Mortgage

Balance: _____

SECOND

Future Value

(from estimate you made in #4 above):

_____

LESS: Future Mortgage Balance:

_____

Your Future Equity: _____

(For more help on any of these calculations, see the online calculator at NeverSellYourFirstHome.com.)

If you're realistic in your answers above, you'll be more likely to make the right choice about selling or not. If you're like most people I've helped, after seeing some of these answers in writing, you're already leaning in one direction or another. Assuming the numbers look positive and that none of your answers are flashing "SELL NOW," go ahead and stop reading and give this book to a friend ☺ or continue on and see if anything else resonates.

Now, let's review your hypothetical purchase, the steps necessary to move, and what's involved in converting your current home to a rental.

1. Why do you want to move and where do you want to move?

_____

_____

_____

_____

2. What's your current monthly payment?

_____

3. What's the price range of the future home?

_____

4. How much home do you think you can afford, and what dollar amount of mortgage do you think you will qualify for?

_____

5. How much money do you think you need to put down on your next house?

     5%   10%   15%

    20% 25% 30%

6. If you do not sell your current home, what are some potential sources for the down payment on your next home, and the amount available from each?

Savings Account: _____

401k: _____

Stocks, Bonds, Mutual Funds: _____

_____

Cash Value Life Insurance: _____

_____

Crypto Currency: _____

Valuables You Could Sell

(antique cars, jewelry, gold, silver, etc.):

_____

Money Gifted to You: _____

7. When would you like to move?

NOW   3 Months   6 Months   1 Year

Other: _____

For most people I've worked with, the first concern about keeping their current home is: How do I qualify for a mortgage when I don't have anyone renting my place currently, and I'm going to have another mortgage payment on my next home? This is the "$100,000 question" but it has an easier answer than you might expect, once you understand the qualifying rules for obtaining a mortgage loan.

So, let's look at how to come up with the down payment for your next home.

I've discovered that many (perhaps even most!) people go to a bank and don't ask the right questions about their loan. What's worse, they typically meet with an entry-level loan officer, and he or she doesn't even know the rules or how to guide someone to do what they want to do. Most times, loan officer has never done something like this, so it seems unwise or too complicated to them (because very few people own rental property, right?).

When I help people accomplish their investment goals, the first thing we always look for is the availability of funds for a down payment. Some people have the ability to draw money as a loan from a 401(k) savings, or they may receive a gift from a relative, or can raise money by liquidating stocks or mutual funds. For most, however, access to liquid funds is not an option. What do they do then?

The next most important question is: "Do you have access to the equity in your home via a home equity line of credit?" Or: "Do you have the ability to do a cash-out refinance in order to draw the money out?" This is not as complicated as it may seem. It just requires some diligence in reviewing your income and debts, as well as the time and patience to set it up.

So, to review your situation, here are your where-to-get-a-down-payment questions:

1. What's the equity in my current home?

2. Do you have access to a 401k, cash accounts, investments, or monetary gifts? If so, how much from each?

_____

_____

_____

3. TRUE or FALSE: I believe that I need to put down 20 percent to avoid PMI.

_____

4. I believe that I need to have my new monthly payment not exceed:

_____

If you've never done this before, it will feel like you're leveraging (borrowing money). That's because you are! But just because you've never done it before doesn't mean you should let it make you feel uncomfortable. You are now entering the phase where the home you formerly lived in is becoming an investment. That investment has asset value called "equity." And the equity in that investment can be used as your next down payment! You can leverage your equity in order to do something else with the money—like buy your next home.

This is one of the biggest benefits of real

estate, and the easiest way to make this shift is either by securing a Home Equity Line of Credit (HELOC) on the property or by doing a "cash-out" refinance on the property. This can become a down payment if your current liquid assets aren't enough to qualify.

The Fun Starts with This Next Step

Your newly converted rental property gives you the ability to generate cash flow and to earn extra income! For most people, this is an awesome moment where the thought of becoming financially free begins. Coupled with rising property values (increased equity from property value appreciation = free money!), owning investment properties becomes a simple vehicle to build wealth.

My own financial planner once offered this perspective on what it takes to become a property investor: "This requires a mental shift. Turning an expense (your current home) that has asset value (your equity) into an investment that produces income is risky. If you choose to invest, you now have risk!"

His recommendations to mitigate that risk were to make it a goal to save at least $2,000 per month if possible, have a four to six months mortgage reserve (monthly PITI payments) saved for each property you own, including your new one, and have other savings in non-401k or non-IRA accounts.

With most conventional mortgage rules, you can qualify for a loan by using a lease agreement on your current home to effectively offset the mortgage payment owed. This would involve some careful timing and, in extreme cases, require you to get a tenant for your current home while shopping for your new home.

The legal terms on owner-occupied mortgages are a bit different than you might expect. Technically, once you live in a property for a few years and potentially decide to move somewhere else, this does not trigger any recall from the lender. So long as timely payments are being made on the mortgage, the rules whereby a lender could call the loan seem never to be enforced. I don't say this as legal advice, but no client has ever told me that, once they moved out of an owner-occupied home and decided to keep it, the lender called and wanted to change the terms of the mortgage or immediately call the loan due.

Investing in real estate isn't especially sexy and exciting. It is, however, strategic. As the exercises in this chapter demonstrate, the figuring might be a little boring, but the payoff is worth it. Coming to a solid conclusion will immensely increase your confidence in your decision.

Remember, too, that as you evolve and age, your interests, your motives, and your income change. Eventually, you will likely "grow out of" your first home. Things you loved initially might begin to bug you. All the items on the initial wish list when you bought the house have now been reprioritized because of your personal growth and changing needs.

If you have moved beyond your home's physical attributes, that's fine because there are always people in the stage of life you were when you purchased it. What's more, your potential *tenants* will be at the exact stage you were when you made your purchase. And for some reason, they've decided to rent, not buy. Perhaps they love the neighborhood, the floor plan, or a dozen other things on their wish list. And guess what? Your current home is perfect for them!

Sound good? I hope so, because now we're ready to talk about the final decision you need to make.

Have Your Candy and Eat It Too

My neighbor was an executive at a very large company and not very happy with his job. I helped him refinance his home and improve his payment. The home was impeccably decorated with a state of the art modern kitchen in a custom home. It featured expensive landscaping, ornate wood throughout, and a pool with water fountains.

A year later, he and his company decided to part ways. He needed to find a job in another city and decided to list his home. As for timing, the market for exclusive homes in really expensive neighborhoods was soft. He initially listed the home for $1,595,000. No offers. He lowered to $1,395,000. No offers.

He called me. He had found a new job in a different city. He was reluctant to buy in the new city prior to selling his home in Nashville, so he found a rental and secured that for his family. I said these 6 words to him... "Have you considered renting your house here?"

Long pause. "You mean...I could do that?" was his reply.

I had experience with this type of situation. I had several clients show me incredible properties that they owned that were now rentals. Believe it or not, one client had rented his vacation home

65

in California for $25,000 per month on a two-year lease (in 2005-6). So I knew anything was possible.

Within two weeks of listing the property for rent for $7,500 per month, he found his renter. It was a relocating CEO from another large company coming to Nashville from overseas. He and his family needed to plant roots and ended up renting the home for two years before they bought.

The irony is that an executive who could make hundreds of critical decisions to run a company had no clue he could rent an exclusive home in an expensive subdivision with HOA rules and committees. Luckily, there was no rule against renting.

The most remarkable part of this story is the numbers. This decision was made in 2012-13. Today, this home is on a four-year lease for $8,500 per month (which is a great deal for the tenant) and the value is up over $1.0 million from the previous attempt to sell at $1.395 million.

Remarkable!

Have Your Candy and Eat It Too

The Facts

Address:
Brierly Court
Brentwood, TN

Property Type:
Single Family

Monthly Mortgage Payment:
$5,700

The Situation

Turn a custom, executive home into a rental property.

Question: Who would pay $7,500 per month for a rental? Wouldn't the home get destroyed by tenants? Where do you even begin with a lease and maintenance?

The Details

Today's Value: $2,592,000

Current Rent in Its Market: $8,500

Mortgage Balance:

2008
Value: $1,195,000
Mortgage: $1,000,000

2013
Value: $1,350,000
Mortgage: $975,000

2021
Value: $2,592,000
Mortgage: $710,000

The Bottom Line

The owners were unwilling to sell at a rock bottom price in 2013. The net worth increased by $1,250,000. The annual income after expenses is $24,000.

Chapter 5

LANDLORD 101—RENTAL PROPERTY BASICS

Do It Yourself or Hire a Manager?

Managing rental property is not something you typically learn in high school or college. And that may be appropriate because of the many things you really can learn only by doing, managing rental property is certainly one of them. And for sure, letting others (like this author) make mistakes for you is the best way to learn. In this chapter, I'll show you how to avoid many of the mistakes that people (including me!) commonly make when managing property.

"No pressure, but I do have another couple who are very interested."

DIY, Anyone?

The most significant starter question you need to ask yourself is this: Are you going to self-manage your property or hire a property manager?

The quick summary is that, if you self-manage, you'll avoid paying fees and potentially improve cash flow. With that increased cash flow, though, comes increased responsibility. It's like you're hiring yourself to do the managing job. So, if you think you want to self-manage, check out the considerations I've listed below.

1. Research the proper amount of rent for which to advertise the home.

You can review property sites such as Zillow, Trulia, Hotpads, Craigslist, Realtor.com, and apartments.com to gauge the average rent for a house like yours in your area. Typically, you can evaluate rental rates by the number of bedrooms and bathrooms, quality of construction, location, and other factors like schools and yard size. Many times, rental rates give priority to a "per-bedroom" factor. For example: Nashville, Tennessee's market in a given area might have housing that rents between $600 and $1,000 per bedroom per month. So, if you own a three-bedroom home, you could potentially charge rent of $1,800 to $3,000 per month. The exact amount within that range will depend on other considerations. As you learn more, you can also spot trends. Even if you don't estimate your rent correctly, the worst that can happen is that the market will let you know if you're off base. No one will rent from you if you're unreasonably higher than competitive properties, and in that case, all you have to do is lower your price.

2. Make sure to have a solid lease.

This is the legal document that will represent you and your interests in the property should something go wrong. Through my attorney, I acquired an eight-page lease for my long-term rental properties. There is virtually no way you can know exactly what is required in a property lease because each county and state have different landlord-tenant laws. You can start to get a feel for the requirements by Googling information about leases in your area, but before you have anyone sign anything, you should contact a real estate attorney or real estate title office and get their input. I suggest calling the title company that helped with your last mortgage deal. Your banker may also be able to help.

3. Make sure your property is fully functional.

This might be one of the most overlooked parts of property management, but you need to be very discerning on this point. Inspect every room, window, door, and any mechanical structures. Also, scrutinize the paint, and see if there are any unpainted areas or marks. Examine the floors. The things tenants notice most are often not always apparent to you—especially if you've been living in the house. You may have "put up with" more deficiencies than you realize. Anything you can do to improve the property so as to improve your first-time showings is crucial.

4. Know how to interview your potential tenants.

Place an ad for the property, and start taking phone calls from candidates. It's essential that you ask the right questions before showing property to a prospective tenant. You need to ask about their ability to pay the rent—what do they do for a job, for how long, and how much their annual income is, whether or not they can pay a rental deposit, what their credit history looks like, what their previous rent payment history is, and why they're looking in your particular area. I've found that open-ended questions work well. For example:

- What made you interested in my property or the area where it is located?
- What's your current situation?
- When are you trying to make a move?
- Can you tell me a little about your employment history?

5. Have a credit application ready.

There many options here. The easiest way is to have the candidate forward to you their most recent credit report (from Credit Karma, www.freecreditreport.com, or MySmartMove. com—a service through Trans Union, www.turbotenant.com).

6. Have a list of repairs ready for your subcontractor when it's time to get them done.

7. Determine how you want to
   collect your monthly rent—by mail,
   in person, online. What works
   best for you?

DOUBLE DOWN

Tatum and Margaret loved their starter home. It was a quirky, older house with three bedrooms upstairs and another makeshift bedroom in the basement. The location was fantastic—an in-town neighborhood with a walkable loop of mixed homes, some updated and newer and some older with neat stone and brick features. They knew practically all of their neighbors, felt like the neighborhood was a part of them, and they never wanted to leave. However, with two small boys and two large dogs, the house was shrinking around them.

Since nothing was for sale in the immediate neighborhood, they looked elsewhere. After a few months, they couldn't find anything that enticed them to move, so they waited.

Then, voila, one of the large, renovated

homes came available—and it was only two doors down!

The house was triple the cost of their first home, and although Tatum thought they could afford the price, it was unnerving to think they would have a much bigger mortgage payment. Even though Tatum worked as a commercial leasing agent and he was accustomed looking at property leases and contracts, his initial instinct was "I think I should sell this place so we can afford the other."

Here's the irony in the story: I was the neighbor in between his house and the one he wanted to buy. So—ha!—he came to ask me for advice. (Sometimes business happens literally in your own backyard.)

I first asked him what factors were important in his decision. He said he believed he could sell the house for a premium, and, since it had gone up so much in value, that he could take the money and pay down the mortgage on the newer, way-more-expensive house. He believed his equity was best used that way.

Although I wasn't convinced he should, Tatum decided to list the house for sale. He closed on the new house with savings for his down payment, spruced up his old house with a paint job, and listed the house for $750,000. Two weeks went by and nothing happened. He lowered it to $700,000. Two more weeks, and nothing. Then $650,000.

At this point, he came to me and said he would not go below $650,000. I said, "Great! Now, let me tell you what you should really do."

And he did it.

Double Down

The Facts

Address:
Parkview Circle
Nashville, TN

Property Type:
Single Family

Monthly Mortgage Payment:
$1,957

The Situation

Tatum and his wife loved their neighborhood, but they needed more space for their family. The layout and square footage no longer worked. Tatum wanted to sell his current home to use the money as a down payment, but the house wasn't selling at the price he wanted.

The Details

Today's Value: $800,000

Current Rent in Its Market: $3,900

Mortgage Balance:

2012
Value: $375,000
Mortgage: $300,000

2017
Value: $650,000
Mortgage: $250,000

2021
Value: $800,000
Mortgage: $250,000
(Inclucing HELOC)

The Bottom Line

The owner's decision not to sell increased the net worth by more than $400,000. Their annual income after expenses is $24,000.

DON'T DIVORCE THE HOUSE

Just after I moved to Nashville, I met a young realtor and began working with his clients who needed mortgage help. He became like a little brother to me—recently married and on a path to becoming one of Nashville's best realtors.

Then came the curveball: a divorce.

He and his wife had purchased a home together and when their divorce was finalized, he remained in the property. Flash forward 24 months, and he was on the fence about whether he wanted to sell or to keep it as his first rental property.

He had found a new home to purchase, and the thought of cashing in and forgetting this house with painful memories was appealing. After a few weeks of attempting to sell it (and a healthy conversation with his "big brother"—me), decided to rent it instead. Now, the numbers we see 15 years later are pretty sweet.

The house is worth three times what he effectively purchased it for in the divorce. At a value of $425,000 to $450,000 and with a mortgage of only about $100,000, his equity position is amazing. His decision, also resulted in about $6,000 per year of positive cash flow.

Sometimes the silver lining of a divorce shows up in interesting ways.

Don't Divorce the House

The Facts

Address:
Benjamin Street
Nashville, TN

Property Type:
Single Family

Monthly Mortgage Payment:
$1,450 (15-year mortgage)

The Situation

The couple that owned their first home together was getting a divorce. The spouse that retained in the property had bad memories in the home and wanted to sell after a few years of living there alone. But, when it came time to sell, the market was dry so, he kept it as a rental.

The Details

Today's Value: $425,000

Current Rent in Its Market: $1,875

Mortgage Balance:

2006
Value: $175,000
Mortgage: $144,000

2008
Value: $225,000
Mortgage: $135,000

2021
Value: $425,000
Mortgage: $105,000

The Bottom Line

The owner's decision not to sell increased his net worth by $250,000. The annual income after expenses is $10,000.

Never Sell Your First Home

_____

_____

_____

_____

_____

_____

_____

_____

_____

_____

_____

_____

_____

_____

_____

_____

_____

_____

_____

_____

_____

_____

_____

_____

Chapter 6

BUYING RENTAL PROPERTY FOR INVESTMENT

How Different Is Buying a Rental as an Investment Versus Converting Your Current Home?

Acquiring rental properties strictly for investment is not for the faint of heart, nor is it for beginners. It takes serious focus and effort to manage your day job while becoming a savvy real estate investor.

"I THOUGHT I WOULD RENT IT OUT FOR THE EXTRA DOUGH."

It's about the Money—Again

I've noticed that clients who come in to obtain a mortgage for purchasing a "rental property" have very specific motives and are extremely numbers focused. And it's a good thing they are. The difference between an initial purchase as an investment versus converting a home you occupy begins with the financing.

Rental properties are known as "non-owner-occupied" (NOO) homes, and mortgage companies consider NOO mortgages a much riskier type of loan because the collateral that secures the loan (the house) isn't being lived in by the owner. That means the owner's ability to make mortgage payments is largely dependent on the tenant paying their rent on time. And guess what that means?

It means the interest you pay on a NOO mortgage will be higher than interest on an owner-occupied loan. The lender also factors in higher maintenance costs than for an owner-occupied home simply because renters may not care for the property as well as an owner would.

It also means you'll have to come up with a bigger down payment. Typically, banks require a minimum 20 percent down, cash reserves of 12 months, and charge a one-half to one percent higher interest rate over an OO home on a 30-year fixed-rate mortgage. The increased interest rate may not sound like much, but over time, really adds up—and all the while, you're making higher monthly payments that cut into your net cash flow.

Why Do People Invest in Rental Property?

Here's the straightforward answer that I've heard over and over: They don't trust the stock market, or they've been taught from one of their family members that real estate is a good investment.

If you've ever read other real estate investing books, then you probably have heard about cash flow and about eventually having passive income. Those seem to be the overriding factors for most. Typical investors are people who currently own their homes, go to work from nine to five in their "day job," and want to create passive income with tangible investments (they like to see and touch their investments versus owning stocks, bonds, or mutual funds).

So What's Different than Buying Your Own Home?

The process of acquiring rental property for a financial portfolio is different than what I described for acquiring the first home you live in. The details to consider and the checklists vary considerably, and since this sort of investment strategy is not the point of this book, I won't go into detail about that.

The amount someone would pay in rent for the condition, size, and location of the home is the most significant component evaluated by the investor, followed by the possibility of future appreciation. If the house under consideration seems great but, for some reason, the cash flow and rent analysis doesn't work, an investor simply will not proceed. Period. There's no "falling in love" with a property because of the way it makes them feel. This is strictly business.

The Pros and Cons of Buying an Investment Property

The biggest "pro" I've seen among my clients is that, the longer they own the property, the more equity they have. Second, the longer they own, the more the Schedule E on their tax returns actually shows taxable income!

There's a positive change when people start to show actual taxable income from real estate on their Federal Income Tax returns. It may sound counter-intuitive to want to show taxable income, but it means that clients who attain this have become much more financially secure than most. They also tend to be savvy about their money, their finances, and their futures. These people are proactive and organized. I call them members of the one-percent club (those with the highest incomes in the US), and they're definitely in the we're-enjoying-our-lives club.

The "cons" of investing are simple. A client once told me the formula: "If you don't take care of your rental property now, it won't take care of you later." This client owns multiple rental properties and believes most people wrongly invest in rental property for the short term. Not getting quick returns from rental property is actually the second biggest downside. Property investment is a long-term strategy.

The third downside is tenant choice and basic property management skills—a factor we covered in Chapter 5. Understanding some of the fundamental elements to finding good tenants and avoiding critical mistakes will help anyone safely navigate the pitfalls of property ownership and tenant management.

Afterwords

THANKS AND WHAT'S NEXT?
How to Contact Us or Submit Your Story

So: Have I mentioned that I hope you don't sell your first home? Or if you've already done that, you don't sell the one you're in now?

No matter where you want to move or what you may fear about leveraging a down payment with equity from your current home, what you wonder about managing rental property, or how much you think life would be simpler with only one house to take care of, if you want to build wealth in one of the easiest, safest, and longest-lasting ways possible. . .

NEVER SELL YOUR FIRST HOME.

I'd love to hear your story or maybe even help you make your own success story. Contact me through the NeverSellYourFirstHome.com website.

I mean it. I want to hear from you!

Appendix

I've attempted to provide as much data and analysis as I can to build your knowledge base. Knowledge is your key to wealth-building. I hope you've enjoyed the case studies in this book, and just in case you'd like to know all the "deep, dark secrets" of my own first home debacle, this appendix has one last case study for you—mine! It's about what I did the second time around.

Russell-ing Up a Big Win

Yes. I know. You know. I sold my first home and I shouldn't have.

So, when we bought our second home in Nashville, I was not about the make the same mistake.

Restored in 1999 by a local developer, 931 Russell Street was an historic four-unit condominium building. After renting one of the units for six months, Christina and I wrote a contract to buy unit D in November 1999 for $169,900. The other units had sold for $169,900, $129,900 and $129,900 respectively, and all of the owners moved in within a few weeks.

For the two years we lived there, we helped maintain the building with the other owners. This "maintenance" took the form of yard clean-up parties on Saturday and other minor group projects as needed. We became good friends with the other owners, and I often joked that if one day they wanted to sell their units, I would buy them.

Living there was a great run, but the cool, walk-up condo started to feel small and inconvenient when we found out we were pregnant. So, we bought a larger home, and in 2001, with the renovations complete on the new house, we moved out of 931 Russell Street.

It was an eight-block move, and it hadn't

taken me a second thought to know that I could easily rent 931, Unit D. Our first tenant stayed with us for three years and paid us $1,700 per month for the privilege.

And then, it happened. One of the other condo owners remembered my quip about buying him out, and he called me out of the blue, ready to sell.

Needless to say, we bought it. And within months, another owner called me. We bought that unit, too. Eventually, we went on to buy the last unit, and now we own the entire building!

As for the original unit D, its value as of this writing is somewhere in the ballpark of $525,000 to $550,000, and the remaining mortgage balance is about $260,000 (woot!). We spent about $100,000 to renovate the property and currently use it as a short-term rental unit since Nashville is ripe with travelers. Our rent after expenses is around $3,000 per month, and our mortgage payment about $2,100.

Our cash flow is roughly $10,000 per year on the property, and the annual principal paydown is about $8,000. Overall, the value since we left in 2001 went from roughly $190,000 to over $500,000!

I may have learned a lesson the hard way, but from now on, I'm not selling.

Russell-ing Up a Big Win

The Facts

Address:
Russell Street
Nashville, TN

Property Type:
Loft Condo:
3 Bedroom 2 Bath

Monthly Mortgage Payment:
$1,140

The Situation

Keeping my next home and not making the same mistake again was a big priority. It was a small 4-unit condominium. Since I had lived in it for two years, I knew its benefits. The end goal was to own all units in the building and begin my rental portfolio.

The Details

Today's Value: $525,000

Current Rent in Its Market: $3,000

Mortgage Balance:

1999
Value: $169,900
Mortgage: $161,400

2021
Value: $525,000
Mortgage: $240,000

The Bottom Line

I chose not to sell after moving in 2001. The property has increased in value by $355,000 and the annual income after expenses is $12,000.

Acknowledgements

Special thanks for all your help, encouragement, and advice: To David Engstrom and "Doc" Engstrom, Dino Rosetti, Martin Bubis, Brandon Bubis, Israel Kirk, Clay Cook, Troy Nunn, Tatum Flynn, Cary Pierce, William Finnerty, Hjalmar and Holly Pompe, Tony Tylman, Chris Parr, Tre Killian, Edwin Peacock, and David Peacock.

Thanks to my team at work: Aaron Senecal, Andy Garretson, Hanna Oatts, Mike Engel, Bob Kraft, and Dean Hackemer. Also, many thanks to my mortgage loan officer friends through the years, and all of the real estate agents, financial planners, accountants, attorneys, and industry people I've worked with and had the pleasure of knowing. You've provided me with answers to many questions and insights that guided both me and my clients.

And speaking of clients: Special thanks to all of you, as well as prospective clients, I've met with over the years. Your case studies truly are the catalyst for this book. Without them, *Never Sell Your First Home* would not be possible.

And many more thanks than I can say to my awesome wife Christina, my mom and dad, my brother and sister.

To my three boys, Patrick, William, and AJ, I hope you develop passion for real estate and decide to Never Sell your first homes! I love you—Dad.

Lightning Source UK Ltd.
Milton Keynes UK
UKHW020659080522
402631UK00010B/498/J